Typing Tutor® IV
with
Letter Invaders®

for the Macintosh and Macintosh Plus

by Kriya Systems®, Inc.

Simon and Schuster Software
A Division of Simon & Schuster Inc.
New York

User's guide designed by Publishing Synthesis, Ltd.
Manufactured in the United States of America
10 9 8 7 6 5 4 3
ISBN: 0-671-66705-X

CONTENTS

INTRODUCTION

Overview

Welcome to the *Typing Tutor IV* keyboard instruction program! Many new features have been added to this product to make it the best keyboard instruction software on the market. Even if you have never used a keyboard before, this program will have you typing with ease and confidence in a very short time. Special keypad instruction is available for anyone who uses a numeric keypad.

THE SPEED BUILDERS—TRM™ and NLG™

To be a consistently fast typist, you need to be so familiar with the keyboard that you type by automatic response, without consciously having to remember the location of each key. Like its predecessor, *Typing Tutor III*, the *Typing Tutor IV* program uses artificial intelligence to monitor your responses and custom design lessons and tests to match your proficiency level. Using a technique called Time Response Monitoring™, or TRM, the program notes the time it takes you to type each letter, then uses this information to create each new lesson for you.

The *Typing Tutor IV* program not only determines which keys you need to practice for your exact level, but also simulates real-life typing experiences with its Natural Language Generator™, or NLG. For truly fast typing, it isn't enough just to learn the locations of the keys. It's important to become familiar with key sequences that are commonly used in everyday language. That is why all lessons and tests are created using actual words, phrases, and sentences that contain the keys you need to practice. Lessons are continuously adjusted to create a pace that is challenging, but not overwhelming. And, as with real word processors, you can even backspace to correct mistakes.

In addition to offering extra practice on slower keys, the *Typing Tutor IV* program is designed to help you learn correct fingering. As each new key is introduced, you are shown which finger to use and are given special drills that help you to remember that key's location in relation to the "home row." Each "home row" finger has a specific "territory" to cover. By revisiting the program's Fingering section and referring to the keyboard diagram in this manual, you will quickly learn the location and correct fingering for every key on the keyboard.

GOALS AND FEEDBACK

The monitoring techniques built into *Typing Tutor IV* do more than create custom lessons and tests. Behind the scenes, the program analyzes the types of errors you are making. This analysis covers transposition errors (for instance, "re" instead of "er"), shifting your fingers over to the wrong part of the keyboard, typing the correct location but with the wrong hand ("mirror" mistakes), or typing a greater percentage of mistakes with particular fingers.

Instead of having to determine your own weaknesses through complex charts and graphs, the program automatically adjusts the lessons and tests to help you overcome specific problems. You are able to concentrate on what you are doing right rather than what you are doing wrong. And you can see how you are doing each step of the way through clearly presented progress reports and graphs.

These feedback mechanisms are important and provide useful information. However, the most efficient way to build good typing skills is to set goals right from the start, discipline yourself to set aside specific times for practicing, and ask someone to assist you by encouraging you to meet those goals. The *Typing Tutor IV* program helps you do these things by having you establish goals and a practice schedule within the context of the program. From that point on, *Typing Tutor IV* keeps track of your progress and offers specific feedback to assist you in meeting your goals.

In addition, the *Typing Tutor IV* program has made it easy for you to assist others who would also like to learn how to type. The program includes a special Instructor Mode and an Instructor's Guide that offers unique features and techniques for helping others develop excellent typing skills. It is ideal for classroom, office, and personal use.

LETTER INVADERS

Learning a new skill is a lot of fun—especially when you're learning while playing games! The *Typing Tutor IV* package includes the new and improved Letter Invaders game. This fascinating arcade-style game enables you to take a break from the lessons and sharpen your speed skills in an exciting way. Letter Invaders uses the results of your lessons to create a game that exactly matches your level of skill. And it reinforces typing accuracy—you have to type the words correctly to get the points! Choose one of two great ways to play—at your present level or with the full keyboard. Letter Invaders includes Word Ships, Boomlets, and two-player competition.

THE TYPING PROGRAM FOR EVERYONE

The *Typing Tutor IV* program has been designed to appeal to people of all ages. Over the past few years, the

Typing Tutor products have reached hundreds of thousands of people in homes, classrooms, and offices, generating an enormous amount of research results. Using this data, the makers of *Typing Tutor IV* have created a flexible system of keyboard instruction to match specific needs.

Although most of the work is done for you in the creation of customized lessons and tests, you can also modify the program to suit specific needs. You can create your own tests of varying length and content and you can concentrate on specific areas of keyboard instruction depending upon your personal requirements. Another important feature is that you can customize tests to any specialized field—legal, medical, scientific, or whatever it happens to be.

In addition to flexibility, *Typing Tutor IV* has been designed to be long lasting. You won't get bored with repetitive typing material because the sentence patterns are generated with virtually infinite (and sometimes humorous!) variety. The lesson material, the variety of feedback, the Letter Invaders game, and many other features provide the combination necessary to retain interest. With sustained interest, practice sessions are easy and enjoyable. Discover for yourself that learning can be fun!

Computer Requirements

To run the *Typing Tutor IV* program and Letter Invaders game on the Apple Macintosh, you will need 512K of memory.

Removal and Care of the Disk

To remove the disk from the plastic envelope (after you have read the End User License Agreement in the back of this book), use scissors or a sharp knife to cut the seal of the envelope's top horizontal edge. After you have made a backup of the *Typing Tutor IV* program, return the original disk to this envelope for safekeeping.

The disk is magnetic and should be handled carefully. Placing it on or near anything magnetic could erase information. Objects such as loudspeakers, kitchen appliances, and paper-clip holders all apply! And try to avoid the most common crime against disks, which is leaving them on a computer or monitor. Although these may seem like convenient places, you may end up with damaged disks!

Making a Backup Copy

Copy me first...

Even though you plan to take good care of your software, accidents do happen. Therefore, it is extremely important for you to create a working copy of the *Typing Tutor IV* Master disk.

...but not more than once.

Please understand that copying this program to sell or give to anyone else is against the law. This includes distribution within schools and clubs.

If you are not familiar with the basic Macintosh fundamentals and terms, you should refer to your Macintosh owner's manual. Follow the step-by-step instructions below to copy the *Typing Tutor IV* Master disk.

COPYING THE PROGRAM WITH ONE DISK DRIVE

1. Turn on the Macintosh power switch. A tone will sound and an icon representing a Macintosh disk will appear on the screen. The blinking question mark indicates that the computer is ready for you to insert the *Typing Tutor IV* Master disk.

2. Insert the *Typing Tutor IV* Master disk into the disk drive. The Macintosh will read the information on the disk and then will display a light gray desktop on its screen. Notice that the *Typing Tutor IV* Master disk icon is present and selected (highlighted).

3. From the File menu at the top of the screen, choose Eject. When the *Typing Tutor IV* Master disk is ejected from the drive, its icon will "ghost" or dim.

4. Insert a blank disk into the disk drive.

5. If this disk is unreadable, a dialogue box will appear asking you whether you'd like to initialize the disk. If so, click Initialize. (You may be given other options. To initialize both sides of a double-sided disk, click Two-Sided. To initialize a disk so you can use it in a 400K disk drive, click One-Sided.)

6. Once the disk is initialized, give it a name. A dialogue box will appear asking you to name the disk. Type **TT IV Working**, or some other name you will recognize in the future.

7. To begin the copy procedure, drag the *Typing Tutor IV* Master disk's icon directly over the icon of the Working Copy disk. Release the mouse. You'll be asked to confirm that you really want to make a copy. Click OK.

8. At this point, you'll need to swap disks several times. Keep up with the messages on the screen and you'll have no problem.

9. Put the enclosed identifying label on the Working Copy disk. Eject the Master and store it in a safe place.

COPYING THE PROGRAM WITH TWO DISK DRIVES

Having a two-drive system greatly simplifies disk copying. You do not have to swap disks repeatedly, as you do with one drive. Follow the step-by-step procedure described in "Copying the Program with One Disk Drive" but make these changes:

- Step 3: There is no need to eject the *Typing Tutor IV* Master disk from the built-in drive.

- Step 4: The Working Copy disk is put in the *external* drive.

COPYING THE PROGRAM WITH A HARD DISK

1. Boot up your hard disk so that its icon or window is visible on the desktop. See your hard disk owner's manual for details.

2. Insert the *Typing Tutor IV* Master disk into the internal drive of the computer. Its icon will be selected and will appear under the hard disk icon.

3. Choose Open from the File menu or double-click on the *Typing Tutor IV* Master disk icon. The *Typing Tutor IV* Master disk window will zoom open to reveal a directory of icons.

4. It is necessary to copy only the *Typing Tutor IV* icon and the three document icons Initial, Quotes, and Story. To accomplish this, drag them one at a time, or as a group, from your *Typing Tutor IV* Master disk to your hard disk. You do not need to transfer the System Folder.

5. Eject the *Typing Tutor IV* Master disk from the disk drive and store it in a safe place.

Getting Started

To start the *Typing Tutor IV* program, turn on the Macintosh power switch and, if you have not installed the program on a hard disk, insert your Working Copy of the *Typing Tutor IV* disk into the disk drive. Choose Open from the File menu or double-click on the disk icon. A window will zoom open revealing the contents of the disk. If this is your first session, double-click on the

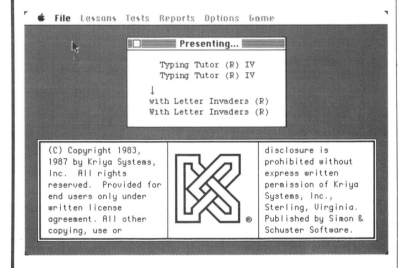

The opening screen.

Typing Tutor IV icon. Otherwise, if you have already created a history file, double-click on that file's icon.

You should now see an opening screen containing the copyright notice and a list of features across the top (this list is referred to as the *menu bar*).

Position the pointer on the menu title File on the menu bar and press the mouse button. If this is your first session with *Typing Tutor IV*, select New Student. In future sessions, you will select Continue Lesson.

YOUR FIRST SESSION

Getting Acquainted

The first step in using *Typing Tutor IV* is to register yourself with the program. After you select New Student from the File menu, you are asked to enter your name so that the program can track your progress and keep a history file of your work. In all subsequent sessions, double-click on the icon with your name to open your history file and continue your work.

As a first-time user, you are given an introduction to the program that orients you to its key features. Then you are asked about your previous typing experience to help the *Typing Tutor IV* program create the best type of lessons for you. If you can type at least 20 words per minute without looking at the keys, choose the Touch Typist selection. Touch typists receive an initial test using all the letters of the alphabet. With this information, the program will know your typing speed on every key and will create lessons to overcome any weak areas.

Goal Setting

The best way to improve your typing skills dramatically is through consistent practice. To help motivate yourself to keep practicing, set a goal of how many words per minute you wish to type. Give yourself a deadline for achieving this goal. Then, before you sit down to practice each time, put yourself in a positive frame of mind that will help you reach your goal.

Because of the importance of setting goals, the *Typing Tutor IV* program asks you to select the words-per-minute speed you would like to achieve. The program highlights a suggested speed range, based on your current level of experience, which you can easily increase or decrease. Then it asks you to select the number of hours per week you intend to practice. Again, the program will highlight a suggested practice time, which can be changed to suit your schedule.

To help you achieve your weekly goal, use the practice schedule provided in this manual and schedule specific days and times to practice. Do everything in your power to stick to those times. The *Typing Tutor IV* program records your time in each session and offers periodic feedback to help you measure your progress.

If your schedule changes or if you wish to increase or decrease your speed goal at a later time, you may do so through the Options menu, described later in this manual. However, please remember that the first few hours are often the most difficult for beginners, so don't get discouraged if it seems a little slow going at first. You'll get better! Try not to change your goals until you've really had a chance to see what you can do.

Guided Tour

After you have set your goals in your first session with *Typing Tutor IV*, you have the choice of going directly to the Practice Lessons, taking a Practice Test, or selecting from the menu bar at the top of the screen. Click on the Select from Menu option.

For a quick overview of each of the categories listed on the menu bar, read the Help screens available from each pull-down menu. Explore the program as much as you want to, then select Practice from the Lessons menu to begin developing your typing skills. If you are a beginner, the lessons begin with the "home row" keys for the left hand: *ASDF*. Touch typists begin with lessons based on the results of their initial timed test.

Practice with the lessons for a while. Then, when you have practiced as much as you want to, select another feature or select Quit from the File menu. If you choose to quit, you will have the option of saving your work. It is important to save your work after each session so that an accurate history file of your progress can be maintained.

The next chapter provides you with a few suggestions for creating effective future sessions with the *Typing Tutor IV* program. This is followed by reference material that explains each of the *Typing Tutor IV* key features. By the end of your first session, you'll have a pretty good understanding of what is available to you in the program and the manual. After you've reviewed the manual and practiced a bit with the lessons, we suggest you end your first session by taking a few minutes to decide how you want to structure future sessions so that you can make the most out of your *Typing Tutor IV* experience.

TYPICAL SESSIONS

Beginners: Your first goal should be to learn the location and correct fingering for the alphabet and punctuation. To do so, spend at least 60 percent of your time in the Practice Lessons section of the program typing practice drills. Every fifteen minutes or so, take a Practice Test to see how well you are typing the keys you have learned.

As more and more new keys are introduced, refer frequently to the fingering diagram in this manual and the Fingering Lesson section in the program to reinforce use of the correct fingering continuously. Always keep your fingers positioned over the home row keys (*ASDF* for the left hand and *JKL;* for the right hand), and reach from there to type any other key on the keyboard. Avoid looking at the keyboard when typing—try to remember the positions of the keys by feel and not by sight.

Once you have learned the home row keys, take at least one good break in the middle of each session for a Letter Invaders game. Hint: You'll achieve the highest scores if you concentrate on using the correct fingering while you play the Letter Invaders game. Don't fall into the trap of two-finger typing—it's a dead end! Also, be sure to select Practice Keys—that way, you'll have a challenging game that uses only the keys you have learned.

Touch Typists: As a touch typist you should be able to type without looking at the keys. However, you may not have reached the point where you can type automatically, without thinking about each key. In order to brush up your typing skills and develop speed and accuracy on the entire keyboard, you may want to divide your time evenly between lessons and tests.

The advantage of the lessons is that the program modifies the material presented to you after each phrase instead of after an entire page of text. The advantage of tests is that you can type continuously for a longer period of time without stopping. Focus on the Practice Tests. These tests are created based on the keys you type well, introducing new keys at a challenging, but not overwhelming, pace. Save the All-Keys Test until later, when you're ready to tackle some of those esoteric symbols!

To make your work most enjoyable, take periodic breaks to play Letter Invaders. Since you know the locations of all the keys, you'll be in for a really challenging game. Go for the high scores and try to reach the top of the chart of all-time high scorers!

Advanced Touch Typists: If you have already developed proficient typing skills on the alphabet and need to increase your speed on numbers and symbols, you may wish to spend a lot of practice time with the All-Keys Test. With this test, you will receive typing material that includes all of the keys on the keyboard. Alternate with Practice Lessons. Based on your typing results, you will be given extra practice on your slowest keys.

When you need periodic breaks from lessons and tests, select the Full Keyboard Letter Invaders game. This one will keep your fingers flying!

Keypad Typists: If your special area of expertise is "number crunching," you'll want to use *Typing Tutor IV* to develop your skills with the keypad. We suggest you spend at least 60 percent of your time with the Keypad Lessons, with the remainder of your time spent on Keypad Tests. A few good sessions with these two areas and you'll be a speed demon on any numeric keypad!

Regardless of your particular interest or level of experience, remember that you can break up your sessions at any time by looking at your Progress Report or at a Speed or Accuracy Graph.

REFERENCE

Keyboard and Keypad Lessons

Practice Lessons is the place to learn all the positions of the keys using correct fingering. With practice, you'll be able to type automatically, without having to remember the location of each key. And you'll develop overall speed and accuracy so that you won't have to slow down for keys that are less commonly used.

The lessons consist of a set of drills that are presented one phrase at a time. Based on your responses, another phrase is presented. Your accumulated results are used continuously to adjust the letters that are presented in each new phrase. New keys are introduced gradually as your speed and accuracy levels become consistent on previously learned keys.

For beginners, lessons begin with the home row keys, *ASDF* for the left hand and *JKL;* for the right hand. The key to typing automatically, without looking, is to practice using the correct fingering right from the start. Always position your fingers over the home row before beginning to type. From the home row, your fingers can comfortably and methodically reach all the other keys on the keyboard. The accompanying keyboard diagram illustrates how correct fingering works on the keyboard and keypad.

Notice how the keyboard is divided into areas. Each finger is responsible for the keys in its area. The index fingers cover the areas numbered 1; the middle fingers cover the number 2 areas; ring fingers work the keys in the areas numbered 3; and little fingers cover the keys in

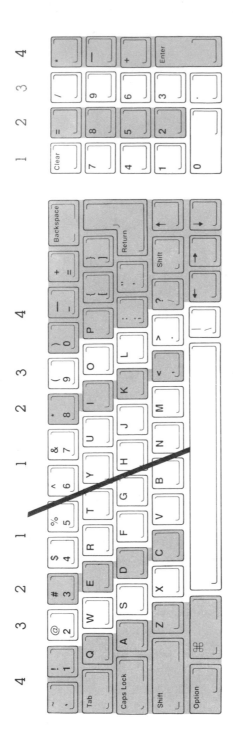

Macintosh Plus keyboard. Though other keyboards for the Macintosh may look a little different and have no numeric keypad, the fingering is the same as shown: 1 = index finger; 2 = middle finger; 3 = ring finger; 4 = little finger. Use thumb for space bar and for 0 on keypad.

the areas numbered 4. The space bar works easily with the thumbs. The Shift keys should be pressed with the little finger of the hand that is not making the keystroke.

Whenever you practice the keyboard lessons, position your hands over the home row keys and type each character that the arrow (↑) points to. Before beginning, look at the Current Focus Keys box and make sure you know where those keys are and which fingers you need to use to type them.

If you aren't sure of correct fingering, either refer to the Fingering section of the program (choose it from the Lessons menu) or refer to the diagram in this manual. After you have typed all the words in the lesson, your speed and accuracy will be shown, along with the next set of words to be typed.

On the screen, an arrow (↓) above the line you are typing indicates that you have made a mistake. If you

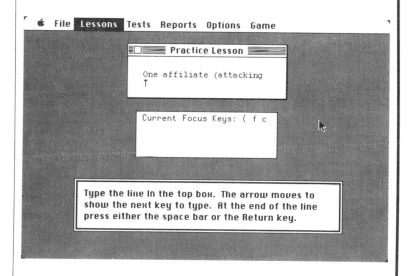

A typical Practice Lesson.

make a mistake, you can press the Backspace key to correct it.

Practice Lesson Summary displays your average speed and accuracy figures at the end of each lesson for the preceding set of drills. The summary also indicates how many keys you have typed above the words-per-minute figure you specified in your speed goal. Finally, it shows your best keys and the ones you need to work on. From this point you can continue the lessons, take a Practice Test, or make another selection from the menu bar.

Keypad Lessons build skills for use with a calculator or any numeric keypad. If your keyboard has a keypad or if you have a keypad connected to your Macintosh, select Keypad from the Lessons menu. You will be shown an outline of the keypad, with the home row keys 4, 5, and 6 highlighted. Position the index, middle, and ring fingers of the right hand over the 4, 5, and 6 keys and reach from these positions to type the 1, 2, 3, 7, 8, 9, and . keys. The 0 is typed with the index finger. The lesson numbers are presented in varying lengths to closely simulate actual lists of numbers. Press the Enter key with your little finger to move from one line to the next.

Keypad Lesson Summary displays average speed and accuracy figures at the completion of each lesson for the preceding set of drills. It shows the number of keys you type over your speed goal, your best keys, and those needing more practice. From this point you can continue with the lessons, take a Keypad Test, or make another selection from the menu bar.

Fingering

One of the *Typing Tutor IV* sections you will refer to often is Fingering. Selected from the Lessons menu, this section shows an outline of the keyboard with the home row keys highlighted.

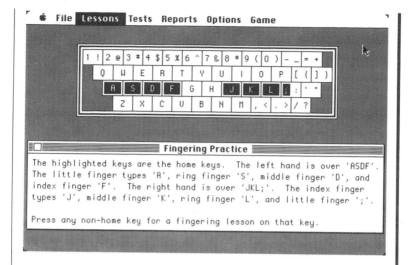

Fingering Lesson.

Press any key other than the home row keys to review the correct finger to use for that key and to receive a home key lesson.

The home key lesson will consist of a series of drills using the key you selected and its corresponding home row key. All of the keys on the keyboard are divided into areas, with each home row finger covering a specific "territory." These drills help you to remember the keyboard position and correct fingering for any key you choose because the entire drill is typed using the same finger. Use this section at any time to help you with keys on which you need extra practice.

Tests

Four different types of tests are available with the *Typing Tutor IV* program—Practice, All-Keys, Disk, and Keypad (available if your keyboard has a keypad or you have a keypad connected to your computer). The Practice Test is based on the results of your lessons. If you are just beginning the lessons, the test will only include the home row keys for the left hand, *ASDF*. Otherwise, the test will include all the characters you have learned thus far, with special emphasis on the keys you type most slowly.

The All-Keys Test means just that—all the letters, numbers, and symbols are used. The purpose of this test is to see how you would do using the full keyboard. The All-Keys Test is recommended for typists who have already learned the alphabet and punctuation and would like to increase their overall typing skills, particularly on symbols that are not used in everyday language.

The main purpose of the Disk Test is to provide you with the facility for setting up your own tests using the content of your choice. Three sample tests are stored on the disk and can be used at any time. One is the initial test that is used to assess a touch typist's previous typing experience and level. Another is a fun and interesting test made up of quotes, and the third is a story. Both the quotes and story tests show you how well you type over a longer period of time—the length of both tests is two screen "pages."

You can add as many tests to the disk as you like (within the limits of the disk space, of course). The tests you add can be as long as you want. They can include anything from legal or medical jargon to inspirational quotations like the Gettysburg Address. This feature was implemented to enable you to customize tests for your specific field of interest. The procedure for creating your own tests is described in the next section of this manual.

The fourth and final type of test available with *Typing Tutor IV* is the Keypad Test. It consists of several columns of numbers and tests your ability to maintain high speed and accuracy levels over longer periods of time.

CREATING YOUR OWN TESTS

Creating your own tests is a simple procedure. Tests can be created with MacWrite or any word processor or editor that can make an ASCII file ("Text Only") without any special characters (such as those used for boldfacing or italics). Simply create your test, of any length, and save it as a Text Only file. The name of your file will appear in the selection box when you select Disk from the Tests menu. (Note: Your test files do not need to be on the same disk as the *Typing Tutor IV* program, so you can create as many as you want on a separate disk.)

Reports and Graphs

The *Typing Tutor IV* program offers many different types of feedback throughout the program. In the lessons, speed and accuracy figures are shown after each drill. Each lesson ends with a summary that highlights your best keys and the keys you need to work on. Each test is followed by a summary in the style of a progress report. It shows your overall speed and accuracy, as well as a breakdown of your speed on letters, numbers, and symbols.

All the feedback you are given in the *Typing Tutor IV* program relates to your words-per-minute speed and your accuracy percentage. Before word processors became widespread, typing teachers typically downgraded for errors and gave a figure called "corrected speed."

Since mistakes are now so easy to correct with the Backspace key, the common practice is to calculate uncorrected speed and report this together with an accuracy figure. Speed is calculated in words per minute, where a word consists of five characters including spaces. *Typing Tutor IV* reports accuracy as the percentage of characters correctly typed. An accuracy figure of

97 percent indicates an average of approximately two mistakes per line on a test. As you gain experience, you should aim for accuracy in the high 90's, and you may want to use the Backspace key to attain 100-percent accuracy.

In addition to the feedback you are given with each lesson and test, the *Typing Tutor IV* program maintains a complete progress report of your work. Choose Progress from the Reports menu for a summary of your work, including the types of lessons and tests you have taken, completion dates, the number of keys you type above the words-per-minute figure you established in your goals, your overall accuracy and speed, and a breakdown of speed by letters (including punctuation), numbers, and symbols.

The Progress Report displays test results first with the most recent dates at the top. Results of a maximum of

⌘ File Lessons Tests Reports Options Game

Progress Report - Robert

Type	Date	Keys Above 20 WPM	Overall Accuracy	Overall Speed	Speed Breakdown Letter	Speed Breakdown Number	Speed Breakdown Symbol
Test							
Practice	05-08-87	7	95%	30	30		
Keypad	05-07-87	3	92%	27			
Practice	05-07-87	4	95%	34	34		
All-keys	05-07-87	26	96%	27	30	15	9
Quotes	05-08-87	33	95%	32	33	24	
Initial	05-07-87	24	90%	22	24	17	8
Lesson - Practice							
Session	05-11-87	7	92%	33	33		
History	05-08-87	34	95%	29	31	20	9
Lesson - Keypad							
Session	05-11-87	0	96%	16			
History	05-08-87	4	92%	25			

Sample Progress Report.

eight tests can be displayed at one time. Of these, only four can be Disk Tests. If you are a touch typist, the results of your initial test will always be displayed so that you can compare them with your current results.

Following the tests summary is a review of Practice Lessons for the keyboard (and keypad, if you have practiced this). Once you have filled the maximum area that can be displayed on the screen, only your most recent data (plus initial test data, if appropriate) is shown. Summaries for lessons and tests are broken down by session and history. Session refers to your most current work, and history provides you with average figures from previous sessions.

In addition to the Progress Report, two graphs are also included in this program—a Speed Graph, which shows your words-per-minute speed on each character, and an Accuracy Graph, which shows your percentage of ac-

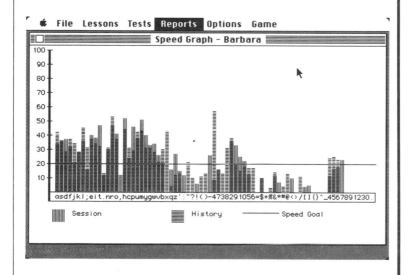

Speed Graph.

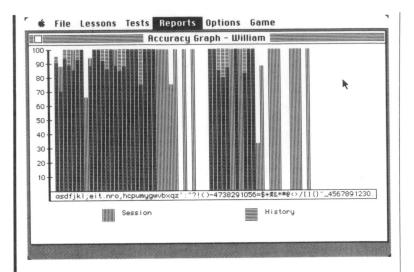

Accuracy Graph.

curacy on each character. Why is this important? It is another way of looking at your overall progress and pinpointing your weakest keys. With this information, you can use the Fingering section to refresh your memory on key positions and to receive practice drills that will help you build speed and accuracy on those keys.

Look at the legends displayed on the graphs—the program shows results from the current session, previous history, and areas where current session and history overlap. The purpose of the graphs is to chart your progress over time. You can see how you are doing in the current session as compared with previous sessions. You can also see which keys you have improved upon with practice and note which keys you consistently type well. The keyboard numbers are shown with letters and symbols. Keypad numbers are listed on the right-hand side of the screen.

Options

The Options menu lets you customize features of the program. You can change the words-per-minute goal you designated at the beginning of the program, or you can alter your practice schedule. It's possible to alter the number of drills that are given to you in each lesson, turn the sound on or off, or even reread the introduction. All of the choices listed on this menu are more fully described in the Help screen for this section.

LETTER INVADERS GAME

Caution: This game may be habit forming! The Letter Invaders game provides a great break from the usual typing drills. Select Play from the Game menu and follow the instructions that are shown on the screen.

Players can choose a game using Practice Keys or Full Keyboard. If you choose Practice Keys, the game will only use keys familiar to you from your lessons. However, be aware that even a Practice Keys game will start out by using *all* the home row keys, *ASDF* and *JKL;*. We recommend that you do not play Letter Invaders until you have learned the home row in the lessons.

If you are already familiar with the keyboard and want to select a truly challenging game, choose Full Key-

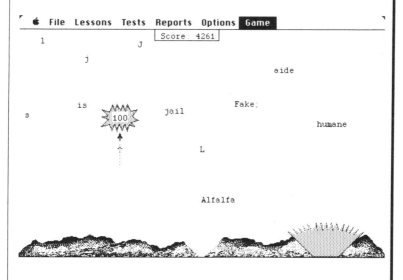

Letter Invaders in play.

board. But be prepared—this game will use all letters, numbers, and symbols. Full Keyboard Letter Invaders will keep your fingers flying!

For two-player games, the second player types in his or her name. Both players compete at the level of the one whose file is currently "opened."

The object of the Letter Invaders game is to score as many points as possible by typing all the letters and words before they hit the "terrain" at the bottom of the screen. You'll be bombarded by letters, words, Boomlets, and Word Ships in many interesting combinations.

Remember to use the Shift key to type capital letters. The game is over when all the terrain has been destroyed. To cancel a game in progress, hold down the Command key (⌘) while typing a period.

The five all-time high scores for both Practice Keys and Full Keyboard games are shown on the scoreboard. You can look at the scoreboard by selecting Scores from the Game menu. Play Letter Invaders with your friends and see how many points you can rack up in each game!

INSTRUCTOR'S GUIDE

Overview

Typing Tutor IV has been designed for maximum flexibility and ease of use in an instructional setting. It is ideal for a school classroom or for increasing typing and data-entry productivity in the office. The history file on your program disk can hold up to eight students, so that students coming to a computer station at different times can share the same program disk. The instructor can look at this disk at any time with the Instructor Mode of *Typing Tutor IV* and review each student's progress, add tests for students to take, and remove old student records. For security, a password is required to get into Instructor Mode. You also have the option of setting up passwords for each of your students to protect individual records in disk-sharing situations.

Your license agreement allows you to have one copy of the program running at a time. Multiple students can share a single disk if they are using the program at different times. For simultaneous use, you must have multiple licensed copies of the program. For example, a classroom that has a computer study area with four computers would need four licensed copies of *Typing Tutor IV*. With eight student records on each disk, up to thirty-two students could be using the program through the day.

Getting Started in Instructor Mode

To enter the Instructor section of *Typing Tutor IV*, start the program as you normally would, then select Instructor Mode from the File menu. The password for entering the Instructor section is **hello**. Type **hello** and press Return or click on the OK button.

PASSWORD

You can change your password from **hello** to any other combination of up to five characters. To change the password, select Instructor Password from the Options menu. Type a new password of five characters or less and click OK, or select Cancel to keep the same password. You can make your password whatever you like, but make it something you will remember! Write it down also, and keep it in a safe place.

In addition to the password needed to enter the Instructor Mode, you can set up all of your students with individual passwords. Select Student Password from the Options menu to display the names of all the registered students on the screen. Selecting students from this list will allow you to review or edit existing passwords, or enter passwords for new students.

Be sure to assign passwords that are easy to remember, but hard enough so that other students cannot easily enter other people's records. Once you have set up passwords for each student, they will need to enter their passwords before using *Typing Tutor IV* in all subsequent sessions. Use this feature of *Typing Tutor IV* only if you are concerned with safeguarding the data of students when a single disk is being shared.

Giving Tests

Typing Tutor IV makes it easy for an instructor to give the same typing test to a group of students. The first step is to create a Disk Test using an editor or word processor as explained in "Creating Your Own Tests." The next step is to encrypt the test. Encrypting a test makes it unreadable except when taking the test by selecting Disk from the Tests menu.

To encrypt a test, select Encrypt from the Options menu. You will see a list of all the unencrypted test files on the disk. If you select one for encryption, the file will be written in encrypted form to the disk. Your original file will no longer exist in unencrypted form, so make a backup copy of it before doing the encrypt procedure if you will want to use it again! If you are using more than one licensed copy of *Typing Tutor IV*, you can copy the encrypted file to other *Typing Tutor IV* program disks.

Students can take the test you create by starting *Typing Tutor IV* and selecting Disk from the Tests menu. They will see a list of Disk Tests, and should select the new test by name. When an encrypted test is selected, it is not possible to leave the test without recording a result in the history file. After all students have taken the test, their results can be reviewed as described in the next section.

Reviewing Student Records

The Reports menu offers the instructor the opportunity to review individual or group records. The choices on the Reports menu are Progress, Speed, Accuracy, Composite, and Help.

If you choose Progress, Speed, or Accuracy, you will need to select the name of the file you wish to review. After identifying a student, you will see the individual Progress Report or the Speed Graph or Accuracy Graph for that student. This allows you to review overall progress and assess the student's strengths and areas needing improvement.

A Composite Report allows you to see a summary of how all students performed on a particular Disk Test. After selecting Composite, you will be asked to choose the test for which you wish to view results. A typical

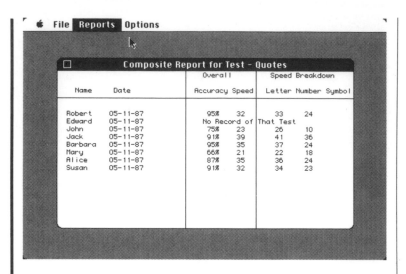

Composite Report for Test - Quotes						
		Overall		Speed Breakdown		
Name	Date	Accuracy	Speed	Letter	Number	Symbol
Robert	05-11-87	95%	32	33	24	
Edward	05-11-87	No Record of		That Test		
John	05-11-87	75%	23	26	10	
Jack	05-11-87	91%	39	41	36	
Barbara	05-11-87	95%	35	37	24	
Mary	05-11-87	66%	21	22	18	
Alice	05-11-87	87%	35	36	24	
Susan	05-11-87	91%	32	34	23	

A Composite Report.

summary is shown in the accompanying illustration. Beside each student's name is the date on which the test was taken and then speed and accuracy figures similar to those in the standard Progress Report.

Deleting Student Records

The *Typing Tutor IV* program provides extra security to protect student files from being accidentally destroyed. Instead of allowing you to destroy these files by dragging their icons to the Trash, as you would normally do in Macintosh software, *Typing Tutor IV* permits deletion of student records only in Instructor Mode. If you need to delete a student's history file, select Delete Student from the Options menu. Select the student history file you wish to delete and select open. This erases all history for that individual.

Restoring Icons

It is possible, outside of the *Typing Tutor IV* program, to drag a student's icon to the Trash and then empty the Trash. Perhaps this would happen as an accident. This would cause the student's icon to disappear but would not delete the student's history; that can only be done in Instructor Mode. If a student icon does get trashed, select Restore Icon from the Options menu in Instructor Mode and click on the name of the student whose icon you wish to restore. An icon for that student will appear on the *Typing Tutor IV* disk window, enabling the student to keep using the program.

Setting Up a Training Program

The *Typing Tutor IV* software can easily be used in a group setting to teach or dramatically improve typing skills. The following information is for you to use to ensure that each participant completes your training program with optimal results.

Whether you are establishing a training program for classroom, office, or home use, the first step is to set up a two-hour group session with all participants. Ideally, each person should have access to a computer during this session. If this is not possible, try to limit a shared computer to two people.

In the initial session you will explain the key functions of the *Typing Tutor IV* software. Begin by taking students through the steps to complete their speed and practice goals. As you will realize through your own practice with the program, these goals can reside on disk for each participant. In addition, duplicate the schedule form provided in this package and ask each person to fill it out. That way, you can enhance the program's automatic monitoring and feedback through personal contact with each participant.

All participants who are able to type at least 20 words per minute should take an initial timed test, and their scores should be written onto their practice schedule sheets. If students are beginners who have never typed before, insert zeros in the initial speed and accuracy slots. You will need to have a basis for comparison once everyone has completed the training program.

It is important that each person set aside sufficient time to practice with the software. Participants should write down specific dates and times when they plan to practice. Although *Typing Tutor IV* makes learning an enjoyable and rewarding experience, there is no substitute for practice. Consistent practice during the first few weeks of the training program is crucial to overall improvement. One of your most important functions as instructor is to follow up with each person to make sure the requirements of the course are being fulfilled in a timely fashion.

Finally, after setting goals and completing the practice schedule form, go through each part of the program with the participants and explain all of *Typing Tutor IV*'s key features to facilitate ease of use. You will want to take each step slowly and emphasize key points, such as using correct fingering, keeping fingers curved over the home row keys, and keeping eyes on the screen—not on the keys! After practicing together as a group for a while, each person should feel comfortable continuing to practice alone. From that point on, your job will be to oversee progress and encourage consistency in practice.

The following are some ideas to encourage motivation and create a group spirit that can help all participants in the training program develop skills to the best of their abilities.

Letter Invaders Contests: Keep a running score on your classroom or office bulletin board showing who has the highest score for Letter Invaders. Publish the name of the winner for the month in the school bulletin or an interoffice memo.

Awards for Greatest Increase: Let all participants know that the greatest *increase* is the true test of accomplishment. Once a week, give a special award to the person who has increased speed and accuracy the most during that week. In a classroom setting, the award may mean extra bonus points and a higher grade. Awards in an office setting can range from a bonus to a free lunch to extra time off work.

Themes: Offer periodic tests using interesting and varied test material. For instance, you can create different themes each week. For classrooms, create typing tests using material that ties in with work in other subjects or current school events. For office use, you may want to create tests on different types of terminology each week, such as medical or legal terms.

Try to create positive incentives so that your classroom, office, or department can pride itself on its accomplishments. Our goal with the *Typing Tutor IV* software is to make the development and building of typing speed and accuracy skills as easy and enjoyable an experience as possible.

After your training program has ended, have a group follow-up session to compare results and provide an opportunity for positive feedback. We hope you enjoy putting this software into practical use in a variety of classroom, office, business, and personal settings.

TYPING TUTOR IV
PRACTICE SCHEDULE FOR

_____

GOAL: My goal is to type _____ words per minute, with _____% accuracy. My commitment is to achieve this goal by _____.

Fill in the times you plan to practice your typing with the _Typing Tutor IV_ software package. Then check (✔) each practice session as you complete it.

We recommend that you practice 30 minutes a day for the first three weeks. Then practice at least 2–3 times per week for 20–30 minutes a day in subsequent weeks.

	Mon.	✔	Tues	✔	Wed.	✔	Thurs.	✔	Fri.	✔
Week of: _____										
Week of:_____										
Week of:_____										
Week of:_____										
Week of:_____										
Week of:_____										
Week of:_____										

Initial typing speed: _____ Accuracy percentage: _____
Ending typing speed: _____ Accuracy percentage: _____
Date: _____ Signed by: _____

FOR ADDITIONAL HELP

If you have questions or need more help, call our Product
Support Center:

(201) 592-2900

1 - 800 - 624 - 0023
800 - 223 - 2348

Sent bad disk to

Prentiss Hall
MICRO SERVICE
200 OLD TAPPIN RD
OLD TAPPIN
NEW JERSEY 07675

Linda Schich
told me to
2/2/89

Important! Read Before Opening Sealed Diskette
END USER LICENSE AGREEMENT

The software in this package is provided to You on the condition that You agree with KRIYA SYSTEMS, INC. ("KRIYA") and SIMON & SCHUSTER, INC. ("S&S") to the terms and conditions set forth below. **Read this End User License Agreement carefully. You will be bound by the terms of this agreement if you open the sealed diskette.** If You do not agree to the terms contained in this End User License Agreement, return the entire product, along with your receipt, to *Simon & Schuster Software, One Gulf + Western Plaza, 14th Floor, New York, New York, 10023, Att: Refunds,* and your purchase price will be refunded.

KRIYA grants, and You hereby accept, a personal, nonexclusive license to use the software program and associated documentation in this package, or any part of it ("Licensed Product"), subject to the following terms and conditions:

1. *License*

The license granted to You hereunder authorizes You to use the Licensed Product on any single computer system. A separate license, pursuant to a separate End User License Agreement, is required for any other computer system on which You intend to use the Licensed Product.

2. *Term*

This End User License Agreement is effective from the date of purchase by You of the Licensed Product and shall remain in force until terminated. You may terminate this End User License Agreement at any time by destroying the Licensed Product together with all copies in any form made by You or received by You. Your right to use or copy the Licensed Product will terminate if You fail to comply with any of the terms or conditions of this End User License Agreement. Upon such termination You shall destroy the copies of the Licensed Product in your possession.

3. *Restriction Against Transfer*

This End User License Agreement, and the Licensed Product, may not be assigned, sublicensed or otherwise transferred by You to another party unless the other party agrees to accept the terms and conditions of this End User License Agreement. If You transfer the Licensed Product, You must at the same time either transfer all copies whether in printed or machine-readable form to the same party or destroy any copies not transferred.

4. *Restrictions Against Copying or Modifying the Licensed Product*

The Licensed Product is copyrighted and may not be further copied without the prior written approval of KRIYA, except that You may make one copy for backup purposes provided You reproduce and include the complete copyright notice on the backup copy. Any unauthorized copying is in violation of this Agreement and may also constitute a violation of the United States Copyright Law for which You could be liable in a civil or criminal suit. **You may not use, transfer, modify, copy or otherwise reproduce the Licensed Product, or any part of it, except as expressly permitted in this End User License Agreement.** You agree to maintain appropriate records of the location of both copies of the Licensed Product, or any part of it. The original and the copy of the Licensed Product, or any part of it, shall be the property of KRIYA. Prior to making any additional copies or other uses of the Licensed Product for instructional purposes, You must contact Simon & Schuster Software and request a copy of a separate site licensing agreement.

5. *Protection and Security*

You agree not to deliver or otherwise make available the Licensed Product or any part of it, including without limitation program listings, object code and source code, to any person other than KRIYA or its employees, except for purposes specifically related to your use of the Licensed Product, without the prior written consent of KRIYA. You shall take all reasonable steps to safeguard the Licensed Product and to ensure that no unauthorized person shall have access to it and that no unauthorized copy of any part of it in any form shall be made.

6. **Limited Warranty**

If You are the original consumer purchaser of a diskette and it is found to be defective in materials or workmanship (which shall not include problems relating to the nature or operation of the Licensed Product) under normal use, S&S will replace it free of charge (or, at S&S's option, refund your purchase price) within 30 days following the date of purchase. Following the 30-day period, and up to one year after purchase, S&S will replace any such defective diskette upon payment of a $5 charge (or, at S&S's option, refund your purchase price), provided that the Limited Warranty Registration Card has been filed within 30 days following the date of purchase. Any request for replacement of a defective diskette must be accompanied by the original defective diskette and proof of date of purchase and purchase price. S&S shall have no obligation to replace a diskette (or refund your purchase price) based on claims of defects in the nature or operation of the Licensed Product.

The software program is provided "as is" without warranty of any kind, either expressed or implied, including but not limited to the implied warranties of merchantability and fitness for a particular purpose. The entire risk as to the quality and performance of the program is with You. Should the program prove defective, You (and not KRIYA or S&S) assume the entire cost of all necessary servicing, repair or correction.

Some states do not allow the exclusion of implied warranties, so the above exclusion may not apply to You. This warranty gives You specific legal rights, and You may also have other rights which vary from state to state.

Neither KRIYA nor S&S warrants that the functions contained in the program will meet your requirements or that the operation of the program will be uninterrupted or error free. Neither KRIYA, S&S nor anyone else who has been involved in the creation or production of this product shall be liable for any direct, indirect, incidental, special or consequential damages, whether arising out of the use or inability to use the product, or any breach of a warranty, and S&S shall have no responsibility except to replace the diskette pursuant to this limited warranty (or, at its option, provide a refund of the purchase price).

No sales personnel or other representative of any party involved in the distribution of the Licensed Product is authorized by KRIYA or S&S to make any warranties with respect to the diskette or the Licensed Product beyond those contained in this Agreement. **Oral statements do not constitute warranties,** shall not be relied upon by You, and are not part of this Agreement. The entire agreement between KRIYA, S&S and You is embodied in this Agreement.

7. *General*

If any provision of this End User License Agreement is determined to be invalid under any applicable statute or rule of law, it shall be deemed omitted and the remaining provisions shall continue in full force and effect. This End User License Agreement is to be governed by and construed in accordance with the laws of the State of New York.

Typing Tutor IV (Macintosh)
REPLACEMENT ORDER FORM

Please use this form when ordering a replacement for a defective diskette.

A. If Ordering within Thirty Days of Purchase
If a diskette is reported defective within thirty days of purchase, a replacement diskette will be provided free of charge. *This card must be totally filled out and accompanied by the defective diskette and a copy of the dated sales receipt.* In addition, please complete and return the Limited Warranty Registration Card.

B. If Ordering after Thirty Days of Purchase but within One Year
If a diskette is reported defective after thirty days but within one year of purchase and the Warranty Registration Card has been properly filed, a replacement diskette will be provided to you for a nominal fee of $5.00 (send check or money order only). *This card must be totally filled out and accompanied by the defective diskette, a copy of the dated sales receipt, and a $5.00 check or money order made payable to Simon & Schuster, Inc.*

NAME_____ PHONE NUMBER ( )_____

ADDRESS_____

CITY_____ STATE _____ ZIP_____

PURCHASE DATE_____

PURCHASE PRICE_____

COMPUTER BRAND & MODEL_____

Please send all requests to Product Support Center, Simon & Schuster, Inc., Route 9W, Englewood Cliffs, NJ 07632; ATTN: Replacements

NOTE: Simon & Schuster reserves the right, at its option, to refund your purchase price in lieu of providing a replacement diskette.

66705-X

Typing Tutor IV (Macintosh)
LIMITED WARRANTY REGISTRATION CARD

In order to preserve your rights as provided for in the limited warranty, this card must be on file with Simon & Schuster within thirty days of purchase. Please fill in the information requested:

NAME_____ PHONE NUMBER ( )_____

ADDRESS_____

CITY_____ STATE _____ ZIP_____

COMPUTER BRAND & MODEL _____ DOS VERSION _____ MEMORY_____K

Where did you purchase this product?

DEALER NAME_____

ADDRESS_____

CITY_____ STATE _____ ZIP_____

PURCHASE DATE_____ PURCHASE PRICE_____

How did you learn about this product? (Check as many as applicable.)

STORE DISPLAY_____ SALESPERSON_____ MAGAZINE ARTICLE_____ ADVERTISEMENT_____

OTHER (Please explain)_____

How long have you owned or used your computer?

LESS THAN 30 DAYS_____ LESS THAN 6 MONTHS_____ 6 MONTHS TO A YEAR_____ OVER 1 YEAR_____

What is your primary use for the computer?

BUSINESS_____ PERSONAL_____ EDUCATION_____ OTHER (Please explain)_____

Where is your computer located?

HOME_____ OFFICE_____ SCHOOL_____ OTHER (Please explain)_____

66705-X

Simon and Schuster Software Division
c/o College Marketing Group, Inc.
50 Cross Street
Winchester, MA 01890

ATTN: Ken Filosi